Join Oliver, a cheerful boy, and Harry, his big mouse friend, as they embark on a magical adventure to celebrate Groundhog Day! Together, they help a nervous groundhog become the star of the day, solve fun contests, and even discover a weather-predicting song. With teamwork, creativity, and lots of fun, they make this Groundhog Day one to remember!

Oliver and Harry's

One frosty morning, Oliver was building a snow fort when he heard a squeaky voice. He turned to see Harry, a big mouse with a tiny scarf. "Oliver, the groundhog needs our help! It wants to be the star of Groundhog Day," Harry explained. Oliver grinned, "Let's do it!"

Oliver and Harry hurried to the groundhog's burrow. "What if no one cheers for me?" it asked nervously. "Don't worry," Oliver said, "Harry and I will make this the best Groundhog Day ever!" Harry nodded, already sketching ideas with his tail.

On the big day, Oliver and Harry decorated the town square with colorful streamers. When the groundhog appeared and saw its shadow, the crowd cheered. "Six more weeks of winter!" it announced. Oliver and Harry celebrated, knowing they made the day special.

The Groundhog

Harry and Oliver were in the woods collecting pine cones when they heard a noise. "Winter is better!" someone shouted. "No, spring is better!" cried Harry. They found a groundhog. "Let's settle this with a competition!" cried Oliver.

Harry suggested a snowball-rolling race for winter and a flower-finding challenge for spring. Harry eagerly agreed. Oliver laughed as one groundhog rolled a snowball while the other dug for flowers.

At the end, called it a tie. "Maybe both seasons are special," Oliver said. Harry nodded, "Let's just enjoy the fun!" The groundhogs laughed, and everyone agreed.

Harry and the Groundhog's Weather Song

Oliver loved music, so when he found Harry humming a magical tune in the woods, Oliver took notice. "This song predicts the weather!" he whispered. Oliver smiled, "We should share it with everyone on Groundhog Day!"

Oliver and Harry built a tiny stage and hung lanterns to create a magical atmosphere. Harry made a twig microphone for the groundhog, who practiced nervously. "You'll be amazing!" Harry encouraged.

On Groundhog Day, the groundhog sang its magical song. "Six more weeks of winter!" it sang, and the crowd applauded. Harry squeaked proudly, "Music makes everything better!" Oliver agreed, laughing.

Oliver, Harry, and the Glowing

On Groundhog Day morning, Oliver woke to Harry tugging his sleeve. "A glowing shadow ran by!" Harry said. They followed the trail to a groundhog looking sad. "I lost my shadow," it explained.

Harry and Oliver searched the forest, asking animals for clues. A wise owl directed them to a sunny clearing where the shadow hid among blooming snowdrops.

With Oliver and Harry's help, the shadow returned to the groundhog. "Thank you!" it cheered as sunlight filled the clearing. Harry squeaked, "Teamwork saves the day!" Oliver smiled, proud of their magical adventure.

Quiz

Circle the correct answer.

What is the name of Oliver's friend?

a) Harry

b) Max

c) Tom

What does the groundhog predict on Groundhog Day?

a) Six more weeks of winter

b) Spring is coming early

c) The sun will shine all year

What does Harry use to make the microphone for the groundhog?

a) A twig

b) A pencil

c) A snowflake

Where do Oliver and Harry find the glowing shadow?

a) In a sunny clearing

b) Under a big tree

c) In a cave

What activity do the twin groundhogs compete in?

a) A snowball-rolling race

b) A dance-off

c) A singing contest

CHHOLST
Groundhog Day

FEB 2 6 2025
PJ

Made in United States
Cleveland, OH
22 February 2025